W9-AVI-717

For my Sister

_____

From

My Sister and Me

Illustrated by Becky Kelly

Written by Patrick Regan

**Andrews McMeel
Publishing**

Kansas City

For my sister Nan. Love, BK

www.beckykelly.com

04 05 06 07 08 EPB 10 9 8 7 6 5 4 3 2 1

ISBN: 0-7407-4152-7

Illustrations by Becky Kelly
Design by Stephanie R. Farley
Edited by Polly Blair
Production by Elizabeth Nuelle

My Sister and Me

When we were very young,

and lost in play
of endless summer days,

I never stopped to think about
how much it meant to me
to have you as my sister.

After all, there was so much to do . . .
tea parties to attend,

trees to climb,

bubbles to blow,

fireflies to chase,

and
secrets to share.

And through it all—
adventures big and small—
we were always side-by-side.

There were never two like me and you . . .
whispering low under the covers
long after bedtime,

giggling at private jokes no one
else would understand . . .
we had a language all our own.

Like any strong-willed young women,
we had our occasional differences of opinion.

But by the end of the day,
we'd always find common ground . . .
and come back around again to each other.

B.K.

When we were young,
in barefoot days,
the world was small and safe.

We learned to share.
We learned to dream.

B.K.

We learned to be kind to each other
and gentle with all God's creatures.

We held hands to cross the street.
We held hands to fall asleep.
And sometimes we held hands . . .
    just to be sure of each other.

Before all the rest, there were just two.
Before friends and school and jobs
and lives stuffed full,
it was just me and you . . .
and empty days that were ours to fill.

B.K.

And no matter what life holds for us,
no matter who we meet,
or how many friends
we might make along the way,

nothing will ever change
those sunny sister days we shared
when we were very young.

And no one will ever know us
or love us in quite the same way
as we know and love each other . . .

My sister and me.